Ostrich

The World's Biggest Bird

by Natalie Lunis

Consultant: Dianna Westmoreland
Vice President
American Ostrich Association

BEARPORT
PUBLISHING

New York, New York

Credits

Cover, ©Franc Podgoršek/Shutterstock; 2–3, ©Richard Packwood/Oxford Scientific; 4, Kathrin Ayer; 4–5, ©Martin Harvey/NHPA; 6, ©Frans Lanting/Minden Pictures; 7BKG, ©Till Leeser/Bilderberg/Peter Arnold; 8–9, ©M. Watson/Ardea.com; 10 (inset), ©Doug Cheeseman/Peter Arnold; 10–11, ©Frans Lanting/Minden Pictures; 12, ©Muriel Hazan/BIOS/Peter Arnold; 13, ©Steve Turner/Oxford Scientific; 14, ©Michael & Christine Denis-Huot/Peter Arnold; 15, ©David Dennis/Oxford Scientific; 16–17, ©Lior Rubin/Peter Arnold; 18 (inset), ©Sunset/Peter Arnold; 18–19, ©Michael & Christine Denis-Huot/Peter Arnold; 20, ©Boyd Norton; 21, ©Fritz Polking/Peter Arnold; 22L, ©Daniel Zupanc/Bruce Coleman; 22C, ©Klein & Hubert/BIOS/Peter Arnold; 22R, ©Jean Paul Chatagnon/Peter Arnold; 23TL, ©Fritz Poelking/Bruce Coleman; 23TR, ©Jim Brandenberg/Minden Pictures; 23BL, ©M. Watson/Ardea.com; 23BR, ©Konrad Wothe/Minden Pictures; 23BKG, ©Berndt Fischer/Oxford Scientific.

Publisher: Kenn Goin
Editorial Director: Adam Siegel
Editorial Development: Nancy Hall, Inc.
Creative Director: Spencer Brinker
Photo Researcher: Carousel Research, Inc.: Mary Teresa Giancoli
Design: Otto Carbajal

Library of Congress Cataloging-in-Publication Data

Lunis, Natalie.
 Ostrich : the world's biggest bird / by Natalie Lunis.
     p. cm. — (SuperSized!)
 Includes bibliographical references.
 ISBN-13: 978-1-59716-394-1 (library binding)
 ISBN-10: 1-59716-394-5 (library binding)
 1. Ostriches—Juvenile literature. I. Title.

QL696.S9L86 2007
598.5'24—dc22
                    2006031855

For more information, write to Bearport Publishing Company, Inc., 101 Fifth Avenue, Suite 6R, New York, New York 10003. Printed in the United States of America.

10 9 8 7 6 5 4 3 2 1

Contents

Big Bird

The ostrich is the biggest bird in the world.

An ostrich is taller than the tallest basketball player.

An ostrich can grow up to 9 feet (2.7 m) tall. It can weigh up to 345 pounds (156 kg).

A Hot, Dry Home

Ostriches live in the **grasslands** and **deserts** of Africa.

They eat mostly grasses and other plants.

Sometimes they eat insects and lizards, too.

Ostriches live in groups of 5 to 50 birds.

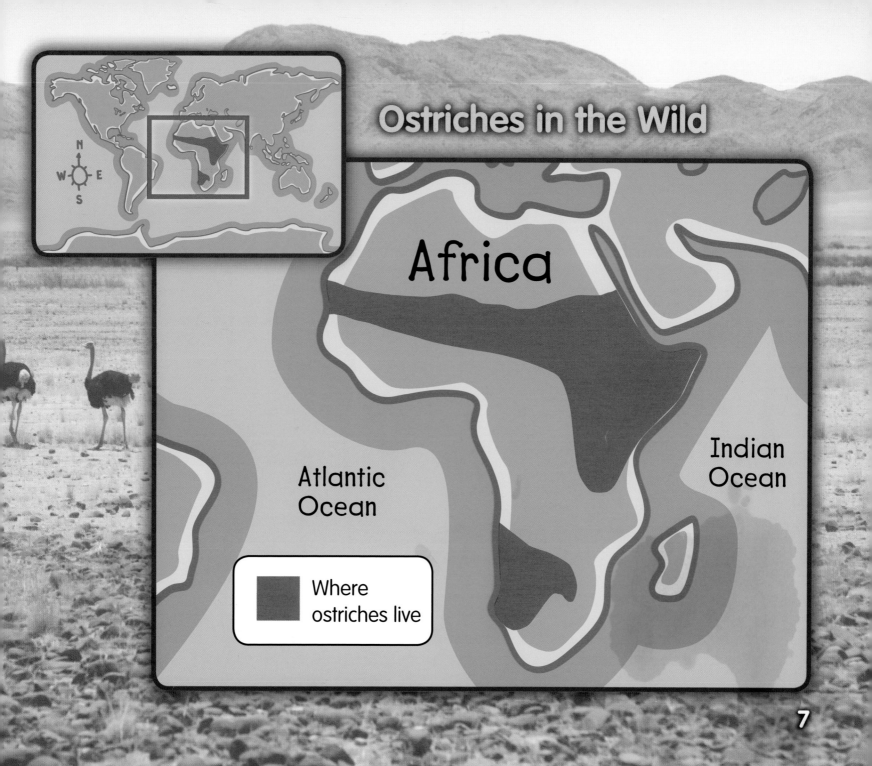

Ostriches in the Wild

Africa

Atlantic
Ocean

Indian
Ocean

Where
ostriches live

On the Run

Ostriches cannot fly, but they can run very fast.

They can run faster than any other bird.

They can run faster than any human.

Their great speed helps them escape from danger.

An ostrich can run 40 miles per hour (64 kph).

Danger! Big Cats!

Lions and **cheetahs** hunt ostriches.

Most of the time, the ostriches get away safely.

These big birds can see well.

They can spot danger from far away and run.

An ostrich has the largest eyes of any animal that lives on land. One eye is almost 2 inches (5 cm) across.

cheetah

Big Feet, Sharp Claws

Ostriches have huge feet.

Each foot has a big toe and a small toe.

The big toe has a sharp **claw** on the end.

An ostrich kicks any enemy that gets too close.

It can kill a lion with one big kick.

claws

A male ostrich's big toe and claw can be 12 inches (30 cm) long.

Jumbo Eggs

All birds lay eggs.

Ostriches lay the biggest eggs of all.

One egg weighs up to 5 pounds (2.2 kg).

An ostrich egg has a very thick shell. The eggshell is as thick as a nickel.

ostrich egg

chicken egg

In the Nest

A male ostrich makes a nest.

He digs a shallow hole in the ground.

Four or five females lay their eggs there.

One ostrich nest might hold 50 eggs.

Growing Chicks

chick

Baby ostriches are called chicks.

They are about 12 inches (30 cm) tall when they hatch.

Chicks stay with their mother and father for a year.

Then they are almost as big as their parents and ready to live on their own.

Ostriches live to be about 40 years old.

Just a Story

Do ostriches bury their heads in the sand when they are afraid?

An old story says so, but it's not true.

Ostriches can outrun their enemies or give them a kick.

These big birds can stand up for themselves!

Ostriches often bend their long necks low to eat. The story about ostriches hiding their heads in the sand probably got started because of the way they eat.

More Big Birds

Ostriches are a kind of bird. All birds are warm-blooded, have feathers, and lay eggs. Most birds fly. A few, such as the ostrich and the penguin, cannot.

Here are three more big birds.

Emu

The emu is the second tallest bird in the world. It can grow up to 6.5 feet (2 m) tall.

Flamingo

The flamingo can grow up to 5 feet (1.5 m) tall.

Sandhill Crane

The sandhill crane can grow up to 5 feet (1.5 m) tall.

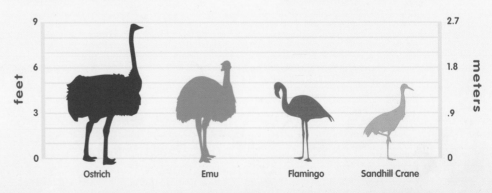

Glossary

cheetahs (CHEE-tuhz) big cats with spotted coats that run fast and live in Africa

deserts (DEZ-urts) dry areas where little rain falls and few plants grow

claw (KLAW) a sharp nail on an animal's toe

grasslands (GRASS-landz) large, open areas of land where grass grows

Index

Read More

Arnold, Caroline. *Ostriches.* Minneapolis, MN: Lerner Publications (2001).

Switzer, Merebeth. *Ostrich.* Danbury, CT: Grolier (1990).

Whitehouse, Patricia. *Ostrich.* Portsmouth, NH: Heinemann (2003).

Learn More Online

To learn more about ostriches, visit **www.bearportpublishing.com/SuperSized**